WARRIOR
MOM RISING

A Mom's Battle Plan to Advocate,
Overcome, and Thrive

JENN ROBB

Need a Quick Win Today, Warrior Mom?

Get your free *Empowering Tips for Warrior Moms* checklist—packed with practical strategies to help you fight smart, advocate boldly, and care for yourself in the process.

Visit **warriormomcoach.net** to download your copy today and start stepping into your strength!

Need to Help Your Teen Cope with Anxiety?

Download *Tips to Help Your Teen with Anxiety*—a free resource full of calming strategies, conversation starters, and tools to help your teen feel seen, safe, and supported.

Head to **warriormomcoach.net** to grab your free copy and start building trust and emotional safety today!

ISBN: 979-8-89694-312-9 - Paperback
ISBN: 979-8-89694-311-2 - Ebook

CONTENTS

FOREWORD

There is a special kind of strength that only a mother fighting for her child can understand. It is the strength that rises in the face of heartbreak, the kind that refuses to give up even when exhaustion threatens to take over. It is the strength that leans into faith when fear whispers doubts. This is the strength of a *Warrior Mom*.

If you are holding this book, chances are you have faced battles you never expected, fought for your child in ways you never imagined, and prayed prayers you never thought you'd have to pray. I see you, Warrior Mom. I see you, and I want you to know there *is* hope.

This book is more than just a story; it is a guide, a lifeline, and a testament that God brings beauty from ashes. It was born out of deep pain but also unwavering faith. It is for every mother who has ever felt alone in the fight for her child's well-being.

But I did not walk this road alone, and this book would not exist without the support, love, and encouragement of many.

First and foremost, I give thanks to Jesus—my Savior, my refuge, and my source of strength when I had none left of my own. Every word of this book is a testimony to His faithfulness and goodness.

To my daughter, Chloe—this journey has been long and hard, but watching you rise has been my greatest joy. Your courage, resilience, and beautiful heart inspire me daily. I am so proud of you, and I love you endlessly.

To my husband—there are no words to fully express my gratitude for you. When I was breaking, you held me up. When I was exhausted, you reminded me to rest. And when I was spiraling, convinced the world was ending, you cracked a joke at just the right moment, somehow making me laugh when I least expected it. Your humor has been a lifeline in the chaos, and I'm beyond grateful to live this life with you.

To my sons—thank you for standing beside me, for loving Chloe unconditionally, and for reminding me that, even in the hardest moments, our family is unbreakable. Your strength, humor, and love have carried us through more than you know. I love you both very much.

To my parents—thank you for your love, wisdom, and unwavering support. Your guidance has shaped me into the woman and mother I am today. Mom, you have been a woman of immense strength and grace, and I can only hope to pass that same resilience and courage on to my own children. Your example has been a foundation in my life, and for that, I am forever grateful.

To my business coach, Brittne Ash—your encouragement, wisdom, and belief in me have been invaluable. Thank you for pushing me beyond my limits and helping me find my voice in this journey. Your impact will forever be a part of my story.

To my writing coach, Allison Davis—thank you for your guidance and support throughout this process. Your insight and expertise helped bring this book to life.

To the Warrior Moms who have shared their hearts, their stories, and their struggles—you are not alone. Your pain has purpose. Your fight matters. And together, we will rise.

May this book be a source of strength, hope, and encouragement as you walk this journey. You are not just a mom in crisis. You are a *Warrior Mom*. And you are never fighting alone.

With love and gratitude,

Jenn

WELCOME, WARRIOR MOM

What do you do when the battle chooses you?

You never signed up for this war. You never imagined your child—the one you love more than life itself—would be fighting battles with anxiety, depression, or self-harm. You never expected to spend nights lying awake, fear gripping your chest, wondering if they'd make it through another day. You never thought you'd have to fight for doctors to take you seriously, for schools to provide the support they need, for your own heart to keep beating under the weight of the unknown.

But...here you are.

Maybe you feel like you're breaking. Maybe you feel like you're failing. Maybe you've screamed in your car between therapy appointments, sobbed into your pillow at night, or whispered, "*God, I can't do this*," through tear-stained lips.

I see you.

I know the gut-wrenching fear of watching your child suffer, the desperate prayers for a breakthrough that feels impossible, and the exhaustion of standing in the fire, wondering if you'll ever make it out. I know because I've lived it.

This wasn't the life I imagined for my family. We were the picture of stability—a loving, two-parent home, deeply rooted in faith. I was a nurse practitioner, and for the first fifteen years of our marriage, a pastor's wife. My husband, Matt, was a worship pastor who later became a financial advisor and mentor. We were present, involved parents, raising two athletic boys and our beautiful baby girl, the one who completed our family. Our home was full—of love, of laughter, of animals (too many, honestly), and of the belief that if we did things right, our children would thrive.

I never thought I'd be the mom sitting in a hospital room, pleading with God for my daughter's life. I never thought I'd have to watch her wrestle with darkness so deep I wasn't sure if she would ever find her way back. I never thought I'd be *this mom*—the one searching for answers, desperate for hope, trying to be strong when I felt like I was crumbling inside.

But here's what I learned in the fire:

- You were not meant to stay broken.
- You were not meant to drown in fear.
- You were not meant to fight this battle alone.

And most of all, you were not meant to lose this battle.

I refused to let the pain define us.

I fought back. I leaned on God, and He met me in the chaos.

And now, I've watched my daughter rise. I've seen her reclaim her joy, rebuild her confidence, and step into a life full of purpose and hope.

Your story is my story.

And, Warrior Mom, you can do this, too.

This book is not just about helping your child. It's about helping you. Because this journey isn't just about survival—it's about transformation. It's about stepping into the strength that's already inside you. It's about learning when to fight, when to surrender, and how to rise—because, Warrior Mom, you were made for this fight.

I See You, Warrior Mom

I see the fierce love and unwavering commitment you have for your child, even as you navigate the challenging waters of severe anxiety, depression, and self-harm. I see the strength it takes to rise each morning, despite the weight of your child's struggles pressing down on your shoulders, and the courage it requires to face each day with hope.

I see your struggles—those moments when you feel lost and desperate for answers. I feel your panic and pain because all you want is to take away your child's suffering and see them happy again.

I see you when you cry alone, when the weight of your heart feels too heavy to bear, when all you want is to retreat into your own space and let the tears fall freely, but you have to keep the family moving forward.

I see you on those sleepless nights, silently watching over your child as they finally find rest.

I see the love that drives you to be strong for them, even when you're crumbling. I see the moments of doubt and fear, and I see the resilience that pushes you to keep going, even when the path is unclear.

You are *not alone* in this journey.

I see you, and I honor the depth of your struggle and the strength of your love. Together, we will find the light amidst the darkness, and together, we will support one another through the trials we face.

But this journey is about more than just surviving.

You don't need another book filled with encouragement that fades as soon as you put it down. You need **a battle plan**—a strategy to help you fight for your child while also fighting for yourself. That's exactly what this book is here to give you.

Every Warrior Mom goes through a transformation—a refining process that turns her pain into strength, her fear into faith, and her struggles into purpose. Throughout this book, we will walk through **The Five Phases of a Warrior Mom's Journey**:

1. **Shock and Survival**—The moment everything changes. The fear, the overwhelm, and the desperate search for answers.

2. **Grief and Guilt**—The weight of *What did I do wrong?* And the lies we tell ourselves as moms.

3. **Equipping and Advocacy**—Learning how to fight for your child, while also learning when to surrender what you can't control.

4. **Healing and Strength**—Finding your own healing as your child begins theirs. Learning to set boundaries, practice self-care, and trust God with the unknown.

5. **Purpose and Transformation**—The final phase: embracing the lessons, finding your fire, and using your journey to impact others.

This journey is not just about surviving—it's about transforming. It's about stepping into the Warrior Mom you were created to be.

I know it's easy to push your own healing aside, to say, *"I'll focus on me later."* But your child needs a mom who is equipped and empowered, not running on empty. Healing doesn't just happen by accident. Breakthrough doesn't come by waiting—it comes by stepping forward, even when the path isn't clear.

So take a deep breath. You're standing at the edge of transformation. This is your journey, your breakthrough, your calling. Are you ready to step forward?

Let's walk this road together.

You were made for this fight.

Scripture Tie-In: Being a Warrior Mom

Proverbs 31:25 (NIV) – *"She is clothed with strength and dignity; she can laugh at the days to come."*

CHAPTER 1

THE MOMENT THAT CHANGED EVERYTHING

(Phase 1: Shock and Survival— The Initial Breaking Point)

The Beginning of the Storm

C hloe was a force of light woven into our family. The baby girl after two boys, she was our princess—not just because she was beautiful and smart, but because she carried herself with an effortless grace. On the competition floor, she pushed herself in cheerleading, each stunt executed with fierce determination, every landing met with unwavering poise. She had a fire in her—a relentless pursuit of perfection, a drive that made her unstoppable.

Her big brothers adored her, always watching out for their baby sister. Caleb was three and Jacob was almost two when Chloe entered the world. They weren't just protective—they were her biggest fans, celebrating every win and standing guard against anything that might dim her shine.

But Chloe's true magic wasn't just in what she did—it was in who she was. She had a kindness that ran deep, a heart that understood creatures great and small. Animals trusted her instinctively, drawn to her gentle spirit in a way that felt almost otherworldly. She didn't just love them—she spoke their language, her hands and heart offering the safety they craved.

Her laughter was a melody, a warmth that wrapped around everyone in its reach. She had a way of filling a room, not just with her presence but with something deeper…an undeniable sense of love, of compassion, of pure, unfiltered joy.

That's why it was so easy to explain away the little changes—like her exhaustion, isolation, and moodiness.

Maybe she was just tired. Maybe she was going through normal teenage shifts, pulling away from us a little. That's what kids do, right?

But looking back now, I can see it. The slow unraveling, the warning signs I didn't recognize for what they were.

It started with little things that, at the time, seemed insignificant, easy to dismiss. Chloe, who had always been the first to bound through the door after school, barely mumbled a hello anymore. Instead of laughing through dinner with her brothers, she pushed her food around her plate, claiming she wasn't hungry. The music that once blared from her room—cheer mixes and pop songs she used to sing at the top of her lungs—were replaced by silence.

She was always tired.

Too tired for practice. Too tired for movie nights. Too tired for the things she once loved.

Her laughter, once so effortless, became rare. When she smiled, it didn't reach her eyes. She would say she was fine, but her face told a different story. The girl who once lit up every room now seemed to shrink into the shadows.

Then came the moments that made my heart tighten. Moments where I would catch her staring blankly at the wall, lost in thoughts she wouldn't share. The once meticulous cheer bag she packed with care sat untouched in the corner. Assignments went missing. Her grades slipped. She flinched at any unexpected touch.

I told myself it was just stress. School had gotten harder. The pressure of cheer competitions was intense. She was a perfectionist. Of course she felt overwhelmed sometimes.

But deep down, I felt it. A slow unraveling. A shift in the air. A whisper of something I couldn't quite name.

And then, the day came when I could no longer pretend it was only a phase.

We discovered Chloe had begun hurting herself.

I remember the way my breath caught in my chest, the way the world seemed to tilt under me. This wasn't just sadness. This wasn't just stress. This was pain. It was a deep, unspoken pain she didn't know how to express. And suddenly, all those little things, the ones I had dismissed or excused, came rushing back in sharp, horrifying clarity.

How had I not seen it sooner? How had we missed the full storm forming right in front of us?

After finding Chloe had been engaging in self-harm, "cutting," I took her to her first counseling appointment. It was Christmas

Eve, 2020. I remember sitting in that office, my heart breaking as I prayed this would be the answer. I thought we had caught it early enough, that if we just got her the help she needed, she would be okay. She went weekly, and I clung to hope that she was healing.

But after some time, I realized she had learned how to play the game—saying what the counselor wanted to hear while still carrying her pain in silence. I could see through it. This wasn't *really* helping.

Determined to find *real* help, I switched her counselors and sought out doctors, psychiatrists, and new treatments. We adjusted medications, monitored every change, and fought relentlessly to help her climb out of the darkness. There were moments of progress, glimpses of my daughter shining through again.

We made the decision to pull her from public school, thinking a private Christian school would provide the structure and positive environment she needed.

Oh, how wrong I was.

Instead of refuge, she found influences that only deepened her spiral. New friendships led to worse decisions, and the battles we thought we were winning suddenly became more intense.

But we never stopped fighting.

We pushed forward, believing that light would break through the darkness.

And then, just when we thought we were finally seeing the light at the end of the tunnel, came **April 4, 2023**.

The Phone Call That Changed Everything

I was at work, frantically trying to get in touch with Chloe. I had called her *fifty* times and texted even more. She wasn't answering my calls or messages, and panic set in.

Desperate, I called my two sons, who were at the high school down the road, and told them to leave school and go home to check on her.

My heart instantly clenched—I just knew.

I didn't know *what* had happened, but I knew in my bones that something was terribly wrong.

My oldest son called me, and his voice was panicked and breathless. "Mom, it's Chloe. She's unconscious. She's not waking up."

"Call 911 right now! Keep trying to wake her up!" I told him, my voice shaking with urgency.

Everything inside me screamed. My body moved before my mind could catch up, keys in hand, racing toward the car.

The next moments were a blur. I vaguely recall my foot slamming the gas pedal to the floor, the speedometer climbing, my breath coming in ragged gasps as I weaved through traffic at over *one hundred miles per hour*.

I saw flashes of worst-case scenarios: sirens, medics unable to revive her, the hollow silence of a world without my daughter in it. I could hear the unthinkable words in my mind before they were even spoken.

I had never felt so helpless.

God, please, I thought. *Please don't take her from me.*

When I arrived, the ambulance was already there. Chloe was being loaded inside, covered in her own vomit but conscious.

Her screams cut through the air, raw and full of anguish.

"I'm sorry, Momma!" she sobbed. "I just wanted the pain to stop."

We rushed through the doors. There were doctors and nurses everywhere. Chloe was still confused, screaming, and crying uncontrollably. The medical team moved quickly, asking a million questions and urgently requesting blood and urine tests.

We weren't completely sure what she had done, but she was alive.

"Her blood alcohol level is *four times* the lethal limit," the doctor explained. His voice was clinical, detached. "She's incredibly lucky to be alive."

That was the word he used. *Lucky.*

I gripped Chloe's hand, willing my strength into her, my tears hot against my cheeks. She stirred, barely opening her eyes, her voice slurred and thick with regret.

"Momma, you don't deserve this," she whispered. "I wish I was dead."

My heart cracked wide open.

In that moment, I saw not just my daughter but every ounce of pain she had been carrying for years. The deep, agonizing pain from a sexual assault years earlier that was unbeknownst to us until this moment. The weight of it pressed down on me, suffocating, consuming.

But as much as I wanted to collapse under that grief, I knew I couldn't.

This was my moment—the moment I would decide whether to drown in the pain or rise up and fight.

A Mother's Unbreakable Love

When we got home from the ER, Chloe was still covered in vomit, weak, and exhausted. She didn't have the strength to care for herself, so I helped her into the shower.

The water ran over her as she leaned against me, her body trembling from exhaustion and emotion.

Between sobs, she kept repeating, "I'm sorry, Momma. I love you."

Through my own tears, the only words I could manage were, "Chloe, I love you more than you know. We'll get through this. Together."

At that moment, she was completely dependent on me—physically, emotionally, spiritually.

She had no strength. No will.

And truthfully, I felt the same way. But...I couldn't show it. I needed to be her rock.

So, I did what I had been doing all along. I leaned on God, begging Him to hold me up when I couldn't hold myself.

I chose to *fight*.

Scripture Tie-In: The Lifeline for a Warrior Mom

"The Lord is near to the brokenhearted and saves the crushed in spirit." (Psalm 34:18 ESV)

If you are in this battle right now, know this: God is near.

Next Step: Take a moment to reflect on the battle you're facing right now. Where do you feel the weight pressing down the hardest? Write it down, then pray over it.

He hears you, and He is fighting for you.

You are not alone in this. You are a Warrior Mom.

CHAPTER 2

WHEN FEAR AND GUILT TAKE OVER

(Phase 1: Shock and Survival— The Emotional Aftermath)

The Guilt That Keeps You up at Night

I barely slept that night.

Every time I closed my eyes, I saw her again—lifeless, pale, slipping away. The hospital room, the doctor's words, her broken voice whispering, "*Momma, I'm sorry.*" It played repeatedly in my mind, refusing to stop.

And then, morning came.

I wanted to believe it had all been a nightmare. Just a terrible, twisted dream. But when I turned my head and saw Chloe curled up beside me, reality hit like a gut punch.

She was still here. Thank God, she was *still* here.

But now what?

The hospital had sent her home, but we were far from okay. I stared at her fragile frame, her breathing soft, her face turned toward me like she was still a little girl needing protection. Except this time, I wasn't sure how to protect her.

How do you even begin to move forward from something like this?

The Lies Moms Believe—The Guilt Spiral

The guilt set in almost immediately.

I replayed everything in my mind, from the moments leading up to the incident to the past few years. How had I missed the signs?

I thought back to all the steps we had taken: pulling her from toxic environments, finding new schools, new counselors, and new medications, and praying over her every night.

And yet, we still ended up here.

Guilt didn't just weigh on my mind—it *crushed my spirit*.

I could barely function. The weight of it all pressed down on me, making even the simplest tasks feel impossible. My body moved through the motions of daily life—work, responsibilities, conversations—but my mind was elsewhere, trapped in an endless loop of "what ifs" and "if onlys." I replayed every moment, every decision, every conversation that might have led us here. Had I missed the signs? Had I been too distracted? Too lenient? Too harsh? The questions never stopped, an internal interrogation that had no end and no answers.

What if I had noticed the signs earlier?

I thought back to the little moments I had brushed off—the evenings when she sat in silence instead of laughing with her brothers, the times she told me she was "just tired." I had believed her. I had wanted to believe her. But now, those moments haunted me.

What if I had pushed harder? Asked the right questions?

I remembered the nights when I had knocked on her bedroom door, sensing something was wrong, only to let it go when she assured me she was fine. *She needs space,* I told myself. But had she? Or had she needed me to push past her walls?

What if I had chosen a different school? A different therapist? A different approach?

Had I placed her in environments that made things worse? Had I trusted the wrong people? The wrong treatments?

What if she had a different mother? Would she be okay?

This was the lie that whispered the loudest. A better mother would have prevented this. A better mother would have known exactly what to do, exactly how to help. A better mother wouldn't be sitting here, watching her daughter slip through her fingers.

That was the heaviest weight of all—the belief that, somehow, I had failed her.

I kept up the act of being strong for her, but inside, I was unraveling.

That's when fear crept in.

Fear of what came next. Fear of all of this happening again. Fear that no matter what I did, I wouldn't be able to stop it.

Fear and guilt are a vicious pair.

Fear whispered, *She will do this again.*

Guilt whispered, *And it will be your fault.*

But here's the truth: Guilt is a liar.

God convicts us, yes, but He does not shame us. Conviction leads to change; shame leads to paralysis.

I tried to push back, to remind myself that I had done everything I could, that I had fought for her in ways only a mother could. But no matter how many logical arguments I gave myself, the guilt remained. It sat on my chest, pressing down until it was hard to breathe, hard to think, hard to be.

At night, when the world was quiet, it was the loudest. I would lie awake, staring at the ceiling, my thoughts running wild. Every time my phone buzzed, my heart clenched, terrified it would be a call I wasn't ready for. Every time I heard the creak of a door, panic spiked through me, bracing for the worst. Sleep wasn't restful. Instead, it was a brief escape that never lasted long enough.

And yet, every morning, I got up and did it all over again. Because that's what moms do. We keep going, even when we're broken. Even when the fear and guilt feel unbearable. Even when we don't know if we have the strength for one more day.

Giving up was never an option, but, still, something had to change.

One night, after another exhausting day of fighting battles I didn't feel equipped for, I sat in my car, my hands gripping the steering wheel, tears streaming down my face. I was empty—emotionally, physically, spiritually. I had nothing left to give. And in that moment, I asked God the question that had been circling my mind for months: *Where did I go wrong?*

I wanted an answer. A moment of clarity. A divine revelation that would tell me exactly what I had done or failed to do that had brought us here. But instead of answers, I felt a quiet, undeniable truth settle deep in my spirit:

I was never meant to carry this burden alone.

As I sat there in silence, I started reflecting, not on my failures, but on the truth I had been too overwhelmed to see. And slowly, things became clear:

- **I was not the cause of Chloe's pain.** Mental health struggles are complex. They are shaped by genetics, life experiences, chemical imbalances, and so many other factors outside of a parent's control. Yes, my choices had shaped Chloe's environment, but they were not the reason for her battle. The enemy wanted me to believe this was my fault, but that was a lie. I had to stop carrying a weight that was never mine to bear.

- **I was not a failure.** A failing mom wouldn't fight this hard. A failing mom wouldn't stay up researching new therapists, advocating at school, adjusting medications, or praying over her child when she felt like there was no hope left. A failing mom wouldn't be consumed with making sure her child got the help she needed. The fact that I was exhausted, that I was breaking under the weight of it all, didn't mean I was failing. It meant I was doing everything in my power to love her through this.

- **I was still the right mom for her, and I was still equipped to fight for her.** No one else in this world could love Chloe the way I do. No one else could be her mom. God didn't make a mistake when He gave her to me—He knew I was the one who would fight for her, who would stand in the gap, who would love her even when she pushed me away. And the same God who entrusted me with this child would also equip me to walk this road with her.

Once I saw these truths, something shifted. The guilt didn't vanish overnight, but I stopped letting it define me. I started fighting differently—not just for Chloe, but for myself. I stopped asking, "*What did I do wrong?*" and started asking, "*What can I do next?*"

And if you're reading this, if you're carrying the same guilt I carried, I want you to hear this:

You are not the cause of your child's pain.
You are not a failure.
You are still the right mom for your child.
And you are still equipped to fight for them.

I know it doesn't feel that way right now. I know the enemy will keep whispering that you should have done more, that if you had just been a better mom, things wouldn't be this way. But that's a lie meant to keep you stuck in shame, and shame has never healed a single child.

Your child doesn't need a perfect mom. They need a *present* mom. They need a mom who keeps showing up, who keeps learning, who keeps fighting. They need a mom who, even in her weakest moments, refuses to let guilt write the story.

So take a breath. Release what is not yours to carry. And step forward in truth.

Because you are still standing. And that means you are still fighting.

And that is what makes you a Warrior Mom.

The enemy wants Warrior Moms like us to feel *powerless*. He wants us to believe the lie that our efforts don't matter—that we are inadequate, that we will never be able to pull our children out of the darkness.

But that is *not true*.

Living in Fear of the Next Crisis

For the next several months, I didn't let Chloe out of my sight.

She went to work with me. She slept beside me. I hovered, watching her every move, constantly bracing for the next worst-case scenario.

I was afraid to let her out of my reach, afraid that the moment I stopped watching, she would slip through my fingers again.

But fear does not only control situations—it controls you.

And if I wasn't careful, fear would consume me.

That was when I realized that my fear, as much as I hated it, was also *harming Chloe*. She needed to see me trust, too. She needed to see that my faith was stronger than my fear.

I had to make a choice: Would I let fear dictate my every move? Or would I trust that God was still in this, still working, still holding my daughter even when I couldn't?

Action Steps: Fighting Fear with Truth

Fear is real.

Guilt is real.

But they don't have to rule us.

When fear and guilt threaten to take over, use these strategies to ground yourself in truth, faith, and action.

Recognizing and rejecting false guilt:

- Write down the specific lies guilt is whispering to you.
- Counter each one with truth from God's Word.
  Example: "*I failed as a mom.*" → "*I am a mom who fights for my child every day.*"

How to talk to yourself when fear is overwhelming:

- When anxiety spikes, have a go-to Scripture, affirmation, or prayer ready.
  Example: "*I will not be ruled by fear. God has given me a spirit of power, love, and a sound mind.*"

Creating a plan for moving forward without panic:

- Set up a structured plan for crisis prevention.

  Example: A daily check-in system with your child that encourages communication without hovering.

Encouragement for the Mom Who Feels Like She's Failing

If you are reading this and carrying the same weight I did, hear me now:

- This is not your fault.
- You are not alone.
- Your child's battle does not define you—it refines you.

The enemy wants you to feel powerless, but you are *not* powerless.

Your love, your advocacy, your prayers—they matter. *You* matter.

Fear wants to paralyze you, but God has given you power. Guilt wants to consume you, but God gives you grace.

"For God has not given us a spirit of fear, but of power and of love and of a sound mind." (2 Timothy 1:7 NKJV)

You are not failing. You are *fighting*. And that makes all the difference.

Next Step: Take five minutes today to write down the fears that are gripping your heart. Then, surrender them to God in prayer.

You are stronger than you think. You are never fighting this battle alone.

CHAPTER 3

THE TURNING POINT—
CHOOSING TO FIGHT

(Phase 2: Grief and Guilt—
Finding Strength in the Struggle)

The Weight of Exhaustion and Fear

The exhaustion was unbearable. The fear, suffocating.

I felt like I was trapped in a never-ending cycle of waiting—waiting for the next breakdown, the next crisis, the next phone call that would make my heart stop.

Every moment felt like I was bracing for impact, holding my breath, terrified of what might come next.

I had given everything I had to save Chloe. Every ounce of energy, every prayer, every desperate attempt to pull her out of the darkness. But, in the process of saving Chloe, I had completely lost myself.

I was running on empty. I was eating poorly, sleeping poorly, barely functioning. There was no space for rest, and no room for self-care. How could there be? Every thought, every action revolved around keeping her safe, keeping her alive.

I had convinced myself that my well-being didn't matter. That I didn't have time to think about myself.

But the truth was, I wasn't just exhausted.

I was drowning.

By living in fear, I was losing both Chloe and myself, and that had to stop. Something had to change, not just for her, but for me, though coming to that realization felt impossible in the moment.

The morning after we returned from the hospital, I sat beside my daughter—still weak, still lost in her pain, but breathing. Alive.

I should have felt relieved. I should have felt able to breathe again.

But I didn't.

Instead, I felt the crushing weight of everything that had led us here: the nights spent crying in my car, the years of fighting for help, the desperate prayers whispered in the dark. I had done *everything* I could to save her, but the truth was, I had been breaking right alongside her.

I had been holding my breath for so long, waiting for the next crisis, for the next collapse, as if my own suffering could somehow prevent hers.

And then the realization hit me like a jolt of electricity: *I can't keep living like this. She needs a mother who isn't just surviving— she needs a mother who is strong enough to fight.*

That morning, I didn't feel strong. I felt shattered. But I also knew this: Fear couldn't have the final say.

So I made a decision. I was going to fight. For me.

For the mother I had been before the darkness swallowed our world. For the woman who still existed beneath the exhaustion, the grief, the fear.

I didn't know what the fight would look like yet. I didn't have a plan; I didn't have all the answers.

But I knew this: I wasn't going to let fear define our story anymore.

We would move forward, not in a reactive, fear-driven way, but in a way that would bring real healing.

I wasn't just going to keep Chloe alive—I was going to help her live, and I was going to live alongside her.

But to do that, I had to step into my role as a Warrior Mom in a whole new way.

Fighting for Chloe, But Also Fighting for Myself

If I was going to be strong for Chloe, I had to start taking care of myself again.

I started with small, intentional shifts:

- **I set boundaries**—I couldn't stay up all night worrying anymore. I committed to resting when I could.
- **I allowed myself to breathe**—I started taking 'me' moments, journaling, and stepping outside of the crisis for moments at a time.

- **I reached out for support**—I wasn't meant to carry this alone. I started leaning on my faith, my family, and trusted people in my life.

I wasn't abandoning Chloe; I was leading her by example.

If I wanted her to believe that life was worth living, I had to live it, too.

Choosing to Trust God Again

I wish I could say my faith didn't waver through all of this, but the truth is it did.

I had prayed. I had fought. I had done everything I thought I was supposed to do. And yet, my daughter had still spiraled into darkness.

Where was God in that?

But here's what I came to understand: God had never left us.

- He was there in the hospital room.
- He was there in the ambulance.
- He was there when I sobbed in my car, begging for answers.
- And He was there in the still, quiet moments when I felt completely alone.

God had not abandoned us; He was holding us up.

And when I finally surrendered my grip, when I let go of my desperate need to control everything, I felt His strength begin to carry me.

I clung to Scriptures like this one: *"So do not fear, for I am with you; do not be dismayed, for I am your God. I will strengthen you and help you; I will uphold you with my righteous right hand"* (Isaiah 41:10 NIV).

I wasn't in this battle alone. I never had been.

The First Steps Toward Healing—Taking Action

Healing didn't happen overnight.

Chloe needed more than just support. She needed a purpose. She needed something that would empower her, build her confidence, and allow her light to shine again. I knew that healing couldn't be just about surviving; it had to be about rediscovering joy.

One day, we attended a beauty party as guests. By the end of the event, Chloe turned to me, her eyes filled with excitement. "Momma, I want to sell skincare and makeup." She was only fifteen—too young to become a consultant on her own—but that didn't stop her. "What if you sign up as the consultant," she suggested, "and we do it together?"

That was it.

A glimpse of excitement, confidence, and something to look forward to. I wasn't going to let that slip away. I signed up, bought the products, and together, we got to work.

At first, Chloe's anxiety was overwhelming. She hid behind me at our first parties, hesitant to speak, observing from the sidelines. But, little by little, I saw a shift. She started applying makeup for women, offering tips, and sharing her knowledge. And when she saw how her efforts made others feel beautiful, her confidence grew. Her voice got stronger. Before long, she was stepping in front of me, leading conversations.

She had found a space where she could shine again.

Finding beauty in direct sales gave Chloe something to be excited about, but confidence isn't built in a day. She was still learning how to believe in herself, to trust that she was capable, worthy, and strong. There were setbacks, of course. Days when her anxiety was too much, moments when her doubt crept back in. But each time, she showed up. Each time, she took another step forward, no matter how small.

Growth isn't linear. Some days, she was full of energy and excitement, ready to take on the world. Other days, she retreated into herself. There were days when her anxiety hit like a tidal wave, drowning out all the confidence she had built. Days when she would wake up, look in the mirror, and whisper, *"I don't think I can do this today."* I'd see it in the way she hesitated before a party, gripping my arm a little tighter, her hands fidgeting with her makeup brush. But what mattered was that she kept trying. She kept pushing forward.

I remember one particular event where she was supposed to lead a skincare demo. She had practiced all week, and she was excited and prepared. But when the moment came, I saw the shift—the way her breath quickened, the way her hands trembled slightly. "Mom, I can't do it. What if I mess up?"

I knelt beside her and reminded her how far she had already come. "Chloe, remember the first party? You barely spoke. And now? You're doing full consultations! You don't have to be perfect. Just show up."

She took a deep breath, and she did it. She stood in front of those women and led the demo—not flawlessly, not without nerves, but with courage.

She was healing.

Not in a grand, miraculous transformation, but through small victories—the moments when she chose to push forward, even when fear told her to retreat.

But some days, fear still won.

There were mornings when she struggled to get out of bed, when the old voices of doubt whispered louder than her progress. There were moments when she felt like she was slipping backward, as if all the progress she had made didn't count.

"Momma, what if I never get better?" she asked.

"You already are," I reminded her. "Not because you don't struggle anymore, but because you don't let that stop you."

And that's the truth about healing. It isn't about never having bad days. It's about learning to keep going anyway.

Even when you have setbacks.
Even when you question yourself.
Even when it feels like you're starting all over again.

Every time Chloe chose to try again, she was winning the battle.

She was finding her way back.

This wasn't just about selling products; it was about reclaiming her sense of self, one small victory at a time.

The first steps were small, but they mattered. We focused on creating a routine—not rigid, but structured enough to provide stability without pressure. EMDR (Eye Movement Desensitization and Reprocessing) therapy continued, and we clung to every small win, no matter how insignificant it might have seemed.

Some days, laughter filled our home again, and I caught glimpses of the vibrant, confident Chloe I once knew. Other days, the darkness crept back in, and it felt like we were starting all over again.

But the difference now? We weren't just surviving. We had a plan.

I stopped walking on eggshells, afraid that saying the wrong thing might break her. Instead, I chose to be steady, to remind her—every single day—of what was true:

- "You are loved."
- "You have a purpose."
- "We will get through this together."

Slowly, piece by piece, I saw my daughter returning. It wasn't perfect. Some days were still incredibly hard. But for the first time in a long time, I had hope.

And hope meant healing was happening.

Action Steps: Stepping into Warrior Mode

Here's what I learned about stepping out of survival mode and into true Warrior Mom mode:

Shift from reactive to proactive parenting:

- Instead of living in crisis mode, create a plan.
- Structure builds security. Set up routines, check-in systems, and open communication.

Set emotional boundaries:

- You can't carry your child's pain for them, but you can walk beside them.
- Learn when to support and when to step back so they can step up.

Prioritize self-care:

- A healthy mom is an effective mom.
- Self-care is not optional—it is a survival strategy.

Speak life over your child:

- They may not believe in themselves yet, so you have to believe in them.
- Speak words of encouragement, hope, and identity over them every day.

Scripture Tie-In: Strength in the Battle

"So do not fear, for I am with you; do not be dismayed, for I am your God. I will strengthen you and help you; I will uphold you with my righteous right hand." (Isaiah 41:10 NIV)

There is strength in surrender. There is power in stepping into who God has called you to be.

Next Step: Think about one small but meaningful action you can take today to create stability for yourself or your child. Maybe it's setting a daily reminder to speak life over them, like "You are loved. You have a purpose. We will get through this together."

Or maybe it's establishing a simple, pressure-free routine—whether that's a morning check-in, a shared activity, or a moment of reflection at the end of the day. Small shifts create big changes. Choose one step and commit to it today.

You are stepping into Warrior Mom mode. Keep going.

CHAPTER 4

BECOMING AN ADVOCATE— FIGHTING FOR YOUR CHILD'S NEEDS

(Phase 3: Equipping and Advocacy—Practical Steps to Become a Warrior Mom)

The Reality of Teen Mental Health in 2025

The mental health crisis among teenagers is no longer something we can afford to ignore.

- One in five adolescents (ages twelve to seventeen) experience at least one major depressive episode each year (Mental Health America, 2025).

- Additionally, youth mental health hospitalizations have increased by 124 percent from 2016 to 2022.

- This report also highlighted a 45 percent increase in emergency department visits for mental health reasons and a 74 percent rise in visits related to suicidal ideation, attempts, and other self-harm incidents (clarifyhealth.com).

- Suicide is now the second leading cause of death among teens and young adults, with 22 percent of high school students seriously considering it in the past year (CDC, 2025).

The numbers are heartbreaking, but these are more than statistics. They are our children!

What is fueling this crisis?

- **Social Media and Technology**—Constant exposure to social media has led to skyrocketing anxiety, comparison traps, and feelings of inadequacy. The pressure to be "liked" and the addiction to scrolling create isolation and detachment from real life.
- **Academic and Social Pressures**—The relentless push for high achievement, extracurriculars, and social status leaves many teens overwhelmed and burned out.
- **Trauma Exposure**—Childhood trauma, bullying, and emotional wounds leave lasting scars. Many teens turn to self-harm, substance use, or withdrawal as a way to cope.

Despite the crisis, far too many teens don't receive the help they need, whether because of stigma, lack of access, or simply because they don't know where to turn.

Why Advocacy Matters More Than Ever

As Warrior Moms, we do not stand on the sidelines.

We fight. We advocate. We push forward when our kids don't have the strength to fight for themselves.

Often, advocacy isn't loud. It isn't a battle fought in doctor's offices or school meetings. It's the quiet, unseen moments when we step in and give our kids what they need most: safety, understanding, and presence.

Advocacy Isn't Always Loud—Sometimes, It's Chocolate Mousse Cake

There was a time when Chloe was so overwhelmed by anxiety, words completely failed her. She couldn't explain what she was feeling, couldn't tell us what she needed—she was just drowning in the weight of it all.

So, we created a code: mousse cake.

And not just any mousse cake—Olive Garden's chocolate mousse cake, her absolute favorite.

It became her unspoken SOS, her way of saying, "I don't have the words, but I need you. I need safety. I need peace." No questions. No pressure. Just understanding.

And every time she said it, her dad or one of her brothers would *immediately* go get it for her. Not because we thought mousse cake could fix anxiety (although, let's be real, chocolate has its *own* kind of magic), but because we wanted her to know:

"We see you. We hear you. You are not alone in this."

And looking back, I see how much this simple, silly system mirrors the way God meets us in our storms.

God's Peace Works Like That, Too

Maybe you've felt it. That deep, wordless exhaustion where you don't even know what to pray. You can't explain what you need; you just know you're sinking.

This is exactly where Peter found himself in Matthew 14.

One moment, he was stepping out onto the water in faith. The next, he was overwhelmed by the waves—fear, doubt, panic. He lost sight of Jesus, and suddenly, he was drowning.

But the second Peter cried out, "Lord, save me!" Jesus immediately reached out His hand and caught him.

Not after Peter had struggled for a while.
Not after Peter found the right words to say.
Not after Peter figured out how to save himself.

Immediately.

Because this story isn't about Peter's failure. It's about Jesus's unfailing presence.

Just like Chloe's mousse cake was her way of saying, "I need help," and we showed up, God showed up for us. His peace doesn't demand explanations. It doesn't require us to have it all together. It meets us right where we are.

And that's the kind of advocacy that matters most.

Being an advocate doesn't always mean fixing everything. Sometimes, it means creating a safe space for your child to simply exist without pressure. Like Chloe's mousse cake code, sometimes advocacy is about showing up before diving into solutions.

But when it's time to step in and fight, we must be wise and intentional.

One of the most critical areas where Warrior Moms must advocate is in choosing the right counselor. Because, let's be honest, not all therapists are created equal.

Vetting a Counselor—Finding the Right Fit

Finding a qualified, effective counselor for your child isn't always easy.

I went through multiple counselors with Chloe before we found the right fit—someone who specialized in adolescent trauma and knew how to truly connect with her.

Remember, therapy is only as good as the therapist.

Questions to Ask When Choosing a Counselor:

- "What is your experience working with teens who have anxiety, depression, or trauma?"
- "What therapy approaches do you use (CBT, EMDR, DBT, trauma-informed therapy, etc.)?"
- "How do you involve parents in the therapy process?"
- "What should I expect in terms of progress and setbacks?"

Red Flags That a Counselor May Not be the Right Fit:

- They dismiss your concerns or minimize your child's struggles.
- They lack structure or clear goals for therapy sessions.

- They don't communicate treatment plans or progress updates.
- Your child dreads therapy and shows no improvement after multiple sessions.

The right therapist shouldn't just check a box. They should truly invest in your child's healing.

If something feels off, trust your instincts and keep searching.

Supporting vs. Enabling—How to be an Effective Advocate

One of the biggest challenges in advocacy is knowing when to step in and when to step back.

Supporting (Healthy Advocacy):

- Encouraging therapy attendance and open conversations.
- Allowing your child to express their emotions without rushing to fix everything.
- Teaching them healthy coping strategies instead of rescuing them every time they struggle.

Enabling (Unhealthy Patterns):

- Making excuses for your child's destructive behaviors.
- Taking over responsibilities that they need to learn to manage.
- Letting guilt dictate parenting decisions rather than their long-term well-being.

Your job as a Warrior Mom is to prepare them for healing—not to remove every obstacle in their way.

Advocating in Medical, School, and Therapy Settings

There will be times when you need to step in, push for answers, and demand change. Whether it's in medical, school, or therapy settings, being informed is your greatest weapon.

Medical Settings:

- Ask direct, specific questions about treatment options.
- Keep detailed notes of medications, side effects, and progress.
- If a doctor isn't listening, push for a second opinion.

School Settings:

- Understand 504 plans and IEPs—mental health accommodations can change everything.
- Meet with teachers, counselors, and school staff—don't assume they know what your child needs.
- Request a trusted adult at school to check in on your child.

Scripture Tie-In: Trusting God's Guidance in Advocacy

"I will instruct you and teach you in the way you should go." (Psalm 32:8 NIV)

You were not called to fight this battle alone, Warrior Mom. God is guiding you every step of the way.

Next Step: Choose one area where you need to advocate more effectively—medical, school, or therapy. Write down three steps you will take this week to move forward in confidence.

CHAPTER 5

PICKING YOUR BATTLES— NO KNUCKLE TATTOOS!

(Phase 3: Equipping and Advocacy—Practical Steps to Become a Warrior Mom)

Not Every Battle Needs to be Fought—But Some Do

As moms, we are wired to protect, guide, and correct our children, but when you're parenting a teen struggling with mental health challenges, the battlefield shifts. Every day can feel like a fight—over school, friends, responsibilities, attitude, and even hygiene. But here's the truth: **You can't fight every battle**. Some fights will drain you and cause unnecessary tension, while others are worth standing your ground on. Wisdom is knowing the difference.

All teens, especially those struggling with mental health, need healthy boundaries. Picking your battles isn't just a parenting tactic—it's a survival skill. The tricky part is knowing the difference between typical teen behavior and a cry for help.

- Rolling their eyes and slamming doors? Annoying, but normal.
- Withdrawing completely, refusing to eat, or undergoing drastic personality changes? That's not just attitude—it's a warning sign.

Esther's Boldness: Knowing When to Step In

The Bible gives us a powerful example of a woman who knew when to step in and when to wait—Queen Esther.

Esther was an ordinary girl who became the queen of a foreign land. But she carried a secret: She was Jewish. When a plot was revealed that all Jewish people would be killed, her cousin Mordecai urged her to go to the king and plead for her people's lives.

But there was a huge problem. No one, not even the queen, was allowed to approach the king without being summoned. Doing so could mean instant death.

Mordecai told Esther, *"Who knows but that you have come to your royal position for such a time as this?"* (Esther 4:14 NIV)

Esther had a choice. She could stay silent and protect herself, or she could risk everything to speak up.

Instead of rushing into action, Esther did something we can all learn from:

- She prayed and fasted for three days before taking action.
- She sought wisdom instead of acting impulsively.
- She trusted God with the outcome, even when the risks were high.

When she finally approached the king, he welcomed her, but, instead of immediately pleading for her people, she wisely invited the king to a banquet. Then another. She waited for the right moment before revealing the plot against her people. And because of her wisdom and boldness, her people were saved.

"I will go to the king, even though it is against the law. And if I perish, I perish." (Esther 4:16 NIV)

What Warrior Moms Can Learn from Esther

As a mom, I relate to Esther's dilemma. There were times when I wanted to charge into battle for Chloe—to demand better care from doctors, to force her to see the truth about herself, to step into situations she wasn't ready to face. But sometimes, wisdom means waiting.

When Chloe was deep in her struggles, I had to learn when to fight and when to pause.

- **Not every battle needs to be fought immediately.** Take time to pray, seek wisdom, and choose your moment carefully.

- **Advocacy requires courage and strategy.** When it's time to fight for your child—whether in school, therapy, or the medical system—step forward boldly, trusting God with the outcome.

- **You were made for this moment.** Just like Esther was placed in her position "for such a time as this," you have been given this child, this battle, and this journey for a reason.

When to Stand Firm and When to Let Go

What's Worth Fighting For? (Non-Negotiables)

Certain battles are absolutely necessary to fight, no matter how much resistance you face. These include the following:

- **Health and Safety**—If your child is engaging in self-harm, substance use, or risky behaviors, intervention is necessary.

- **Therapy and Treatment Compliance**—Mental health treatment is not optional. If your child is resistant, find creative ways to make it non-negotiable.

- **Basic Responsibilities and Respect**—Teaching them to be accountable for schoolwork and chores and to respect others is part of preparing them for adulthood.

What Can be Let Go? (Things That Won't Matter in Five Years)

Not every battle is worth your energy. Some arguments will only push your child away and create unnecessary conflict. These issues may not be worth the fight:

- **Hair Color and Clothing Choices**—Expression is part of your child's autonomy. Let them explore (within reason).

- **Music and Entertainment Preferences**—Unless it's promoting harmful behaviors, let them have their space.

- **Social Quirks and Moods**—Teens are emotional. Not every eye roll requires a lecture.

I learned this lesson firsthand when Chloe, in the depths of her struggles, decided she wanted bleach-blonde hair, dark clothing, and moody aesthetics. Fine, whatever. Pick your battles, right?

But then came the knuckle tattoos. Sweet mercy, *no*. That was a battle I fought without hesitation. I had visions of her getting NO REGERTS tattooed across her hands—I mean, can you imagine? Teenage decisions are already questionable enough without misspelled *regret* permanently inked onto her knuckles.

She was thirteen, for crying out loud! That was my hard line in the sand. To this day, she thanks me for it. Turns out that sometimes moms really do know best—even if it takes a few years and a little common sense for your children to admit it.

Setting Healthy Boundaries Without Breaking Their Spirit

Fighting for the right things isn't about control. It's about guidance. When you set boundaries, they should feel firm but loving, not suffocating.

How to Set Boundaries That Work:

- **Be clear and consistent**—If a rule is important, enforce it consistently.
- **Allow natural consequences**—Some lessons can only be learned "the hard way," through experience.
- **Give them autonomy where possible**—Let them have choices in areas that won't cause harm.

Action Step: The Three-Question Rule for Deciding a Battle

Before engaging in a power struggle, ask yourself these questions:

1. "Does this impact my child's safety or well-being?"
2. "Will this matter in five years?"
3. "Is this about control, or is it about genuine concern?"

If you can't confidently say it's worth the fight, *let it go.*

Scripture Tie-In: Guarding Your Heart and Choosing Wisdom

"Above all else, guard your heart, for everything you do flows from it." (Proverbs 4:23 NIV)

Parenting a struggling teen requires wisdom, patience, and grace. Guarding your heart means knowing where to invest your energy and when to surrender control to God. You are their protector, not their dictator.

Choose your battles, Warrior Mom—you are fighting for the long game.

Next Step: Identify one battle you've been fighting that you need to let go of and one that requires you to stand firm. Write down an action plan for each.

CHAPTER 6

FAITH OVER FEAR—SURRENDERING YOUR CHILD TO GOD

(Phase 3: Equipping and Advocacy— Practical Steps to Become a Warrior Mom)

The Hardest Lesson: You Can't Control Everything

As Warrior Moms, we are fierce defenders. We fight for our children, stand guard over their well-being, and do everything in our power to shield them from pain. But no matter how hard we try, we eventually come face to face with a difficult truth:

We cannot control everything.

No matter how much we fight, plan, or protect, there are battles that only God can fight for our children. Surrendering your child to God is one of the hardest yet most powerful things you will ever do as a mother.

Hannah's Story: A Mother's Surrender

Hannah's story in 1 Samuel 1–2 is a powerful example of what it means to trust God completely with your child.

Hannah was a woman who deeply longed for a child, but, year after year, she remained barren. To make things worse, she was taunted and ridiculed by her husband's other wife, Peninnah, who had many children.

Hannah wept bitterly, feeling forgotten and broken. But instead of allowing despair to consume her, Hannah turned to God in prayer. *"Lord Almighty, if you will only look on your servant's misery and remember me, and not forget your servant but give her a son, then I will give him to the Lord for all the days of his life"* (1 Samuel 1:11 NIV).

Hannah surrendered before she saw the answer.

She prayed with total faith, believing that God would hear her. And He did. Not long after, Hannah conceived and gave birth to Samuel.

But her story didn't end there.

Hannah kept her vow. When Samuel was still a young child, she brought him to the temple and dedicated him fully to God.

"I prayed for this child, and the Lord has granted me what I asked of Him. So now I give him to the Lord." (1 Samuel 1:27–28 NIV)

Imagine how hard that must have been—after longing for a child for so long, she had to let him go.

But Hannah trusted that God loved Samuel even more than she did. She knew Samuel's purpose was in God's hands, not hers.

What Hannah's Story Teaches us About Letting Go

- **Surrendering does not mean giving up.** It means trusting that God is writing a greater story than we can see.
- **God loves our children even more than we do.** When we place them in His hands, we are entrusting them to the safest place they can be.
- **True peace comes when we release control.** Hannah left her prayer with peace, knowing that God was faithful.

When I finally surrendered Chloe to God, I thought of Hannah. I realized I had spent so much time carrying a burden that was never mine to carry alone.

Hannah's story reminds us that God is in control—even when we don't see the whole picture.

The Moment I Had to Let Go

I was beyond exhausted. I was physically, emotionally, and spiritually drained. Every instinct told me to hold on tighter, to do more, to try harder. But what I didn't see then was that my relentless grip on control wasn't saving us.

I was drowning in fear. Chloe was drowning in pain. We were both grasping at anything to stay afloat.

Then came the day that changed everything.

The day I found Chloe unresponsive.

The day I broke the speed limit racing to her.

The day I sat in a sterile hospital room, covered in my daughter's vomit, holding her shaking hands and hearing her whisper, *"Momma, I'm sorry. I just wanted the pain to stop."*

That night, as I sobbed, pleading with God, a truth I had been resisting finally hit me:

I couldn't fix this. I never could.

I had been carrying a burden that was never mine to bear alone. And in that moment, I made the hardest decision of my life. I surrendered her to God.

Letting go isn't giving up. It's trusting God to do what only He can do.

The Hidden Battles of a Warrior Mom

Parenting a child battling anxiety, depression, or trauma is an emotional battlefield.

Some days, you see glimpses of progress.
Other days, you're just trying to keep breathing.

The constant worry, fear, and exhaustion can leave you completely drained. And even when you're fighting with everything you have, it can still feel like you're losing ground.

Here's what Warrior Moms are struggling with:

- **Feeling helpless**—Watching your child suffer and not knowing how to fix it.

- **Guilt and self-blame**—Wondering how you missed the signs and questioning what you did wrong.
- **Walking on eggshells**—Fearing that one wrong word will send them spiraling.
- **Navigating a broken system**—Fighting for the right doctors, therapists, and treatments when nothing seems to be working.
- **Balancing life while advocating**—Juggling work, other children, relationships, and self-care while still being in fight mode 24/7.

And yet, we keep going. Because we love our children with a force that refuses to give up.

But, Warrior Mom, hear me: You were never meant to fight this battle alone. You are not failing. You are not powerless. You are being refined in the fire, and there is hope beyond the exhaustion.

God Was Fighting for Me, Too

I thought I was the one fighting for Chloe, but what I didn't realize was God was fighting for me.

Just as Chloe resisted my help, I had to stop and ask myself:

- *How many times have I resisted God?*
- *How often have I pulled away, convinced I could handle things on my own?*
- *How many times have I ignored His guidance because I was too determined to fix everything my way?*

God was teaching me something I desperately needed to understand: Just as He is patient, steady, and unwavering in His love for me, I needed to be the same for Chloe.

No matter how much she pushed me away, I refused to leave her side. And no matter how much I pushed God away, He never left mine.

Surrendering Chloe to God didn't just change her journey. It also changed mine.

I learned to trust Him in ways I never had before. I learned that He is my rock, my refuge, my steady hand in the storm. And I learned that no matter how chaotic life feels…

God remains unshaken.

Next Step: Trusting God with Your Child

Write out your own personal prayer of surrender. Take five minutes today to release your fears to God and trust Him with your child's future.

You don't have to carry this alone anymore. He's got them. And He's got you, too.

CHAPTER 7

SELF-CARE IS NOT SELFISH—
WHY YOUR HEALING MATTERS

(Phase 4: Healing and Strength—Practical Steps to Become a Warrior Mom)

The Burnout Moment: When I Realized I Couldn't Pour from an Empty Cup

I wear a lot of hats: nurse practitioner, direct sales leader (because I love it and believe in it wholeheartedly), wife, and mother to three teenagers who are constantly juggling a million things at once.

And honestly? I thrive in chaos.

Chaos isn't just something I manage. It's where I'm wired to excel. I was trained in the ER, trauma, and critical care, where split-second decisions meant the difference between life and death. Chaos was my middle name. I was alive when I was running two codes simultaneously, handling life-threatening emergencies, placing a chest tube and a central line—all at the same time. Pressure didn't break me; it *fueled* me.

I'm the kind of person who takes on a full plate, then piles on more, convinced I can handle it all because, well…I usually do.

But handling it all didn't mean it wasn't heavy.

I was the glue that held everything together—coordinating schedules, managing responsibilities, making sure everyone had what they needed, and keeping the household running. Whether it was planning trips, tracking appointments, or making last-minute adjustments to keep life on course, I was the leader.

Go, Team Robb!

But even the strongest leaders can only carry so much before the weight becomes unbearable.

The Weight of Carrying it All

Now, let's be clear. I was not alone on this journey.

My husband of twenty-five years was always by my side, loving Chloe deeply and supporting me through every step. My two sons—Chloe's big brothers, Caleb and Jacob—also stepped up in ways that still make me emotional. They didn't always have the perfect words, but they knew how to show up for their sister in the ways that mattered: They brought her chocolate mousse cake from Olive Garden (because they knew the way to her heart). They took her to the zoo, to the movies, bowling, or out to eat, giving her moments of joy and connection even in the hardest times.

Even so, I was running myself into the ground because I am *Mom*!

Every waking moment was spent making sure Chloe was safe while balancing multiple roles—being her mom, her advocate, and her beauty business partner, on top of managing my own career as a nurse practitioner and direct sales agent.

Chloe and I had built something special together with our direct sales business, and we were hitting major milestones.

She was thriving: gaining confidence, pouring herself into competitive cheer, and pushing herself to master new skills.

And me? Well, I was so consumed with keeping everything afloat that I forgot to refill my own cup.

I told myself, *Just keep going. Hold it all together. You don't have time to stop.*

Until one day…I crashed.

The Breaking Point—When I Had Nothing Left to Give

I still remember the exact moment I broke down.

I was sitting in my car when I started sobbing uncontrollably, feeling like I had nothing left to give.

I was:

- Depleted—physically, emotionally, mentally.
- Running on fumes, trying to be everything for everyone.
- Holding on to the last shred of strength I had left.

And then, God whispered to my heart: *"You can't do this without Me."*

That was it.

I had been trying to be *everything* for Chloe.

But I wasn't meant to fight this battle alone.

God had always been there, waiting for me to:

- Lean into Him.
- Let Him renew my strength.
- Trust that I wasn't just a mother—I was His daughter, too.

That day, I realized a truth that changed everything:

Self-care isn't about stepping away from my role as a mother. It's about equipping myself to show up even stronger.

What Self-Care is and Why it Matters

Self-care is not selfish—it is essential.

It is the intentional practice of tending to your own well-being— physically, emotionally, mentally, and spiritually—so that you can show up fully for yourself and your family.

It's not an escape. It's a strategy.

Neglecting self-care leads to multiple problems:

- **Burnout**—Running on fumes, constantly feeling exhausted, and being emotionally drained.
- **Irritability**—Snapping at your family, struggling with patience, and feeling overwhelmed.
- **Loss of self-identity**—Forgetting who you are outside of being a mom and caregiver.

And let's be honest, when moms are burnt out, the whole family feels it.

The Example You Set Matters

Practicing self-care models healthy coping mechanisms for your children.

They learn from what you do, not just what you say.

If they see you running yourself ragged, constantly stressed, and never taking a break, they learn that exhaustion is the standard. But if they see you setting boundaries, feeling joy, and prioritizing your well-being, they learn that strength comes from balance, not burnout.

Your actions will always speak louder than your words. Taking care of yourself is not just for you—it's for your child, too.

Action Step: Create Your Own Self-Care Plan

Take five minutes to map out your self-care action plan:

- **Mind**—How will you protect your mental health this week (e.g., journaling, reading, therapy, quiet time)?
- **Body**—What will you do to take care of your physical health (e.g., movement, sleep, hydration)?
- **Spirit**—How will you strengthen your faith (e.g., prayer, worship, Scripture, community)?

Identify obstacles that keep you from prioritizing yourself and make a plan to overcome them. What's one small step you can take today?

Scripture Tie-In: Finding Strength in Rest

"But those who hope in the Lord will renew their strength. They will soar on wings like eagles; they will run and not grow weary, they will walk and not be faint." (Isaiah 40:31 NIV)

Warrior Mom, you don't have to run on empty.

God calls us to rest, renew, and take care of ourselves. Because we cannot fight this battle well if we are constantly running on empty.

Remember, self-care is not selfish—it's *essential*.

Next Step:

Choose *one* self-care action step today and commit to it. Write it down or set a reminder if you have to.

It's time to start pouring into yourself, too.

CHAPTER 8

REFINEMENT IN THE FIRE—GOD USES OUR PAIN FOR A PURPOSE

(Phase 5: Purpose and Transformation—The Transformation and Coaching Connection)

The Fire That Refines Us

Pain has a way of making us feel broken, weak, and overwhelmed.

But in God's hands, pain becomes a tool of transformation.

Think about gold being refined in fire. It must go through intense heat to remove impurities, making it stronger, more radiant, and more valuable.

That's what this journey has been doing in you, Warrior Mom. The fire wasn't meant to destroy you—it was meant to refine you.

I never thought I'd survive some of the moments we faced with Chloe:

- The nights I lay awake, terrified for her future.
- The days I fought back tears just to get through work.
- The moments I questioned if I had the strength to keep going.

But looking back now, I see it…God was refining me.

Every battle taught me resilience. Every heartbreak deepened my compassion. Every prayer stretched my faith.

There were times I wanted to throw my hands up and say, "I can't do this anymore."

But somehow, God kept pulling me forward, showing me that this fire was burning away my fears, my doubts, and the belief that I had to have everything under control.

Because here's the truth: I was never in control to begin with.

The Fiery Furnace of Glassblowing—A Family Experience

I've always been fascinated by glassblowing.

There's something mesmerizing about watching broken, jagged pieces of glass get thrown into a fiery furnace, heated until they completely transform, and then shaped into something breathtakingly beautiful.

On one of our family vacations to Park City, Utah, we had the chance to experience this firsthand.

We signed up for a glassblowing class, and let me tell you…It was hot. It was intense. And it was slightly terrifying!

(Kind of like parenting a teenager.)

From Broken Pieces to Beauty

The process was incredible.

We started with scraps of broken glass—random, sharp, and unusable on their own. Then, we watched as they were placed in a 2,000-degree furnace and started melting together, transforming into something new.

Chloe was captivated.

As she shaped her bowl, her face lit up, her eyes reflecting the fiery glow of the furnace.

She chose multiple colors, blending them together into a swirling masterpiece.

What started as broken, discarded glass became something beautiful and whole.

That bowl sits on our table today—a constant reminder that **beauty can come from brokenness**.

God's Refining Fire

This is exactly what God does with us.

We are those shattered pieces, sometimes feeling:

- Too broken to be useful.
- Too hurt to be whole.
- Too lost to ever be found again.

But in His hands, through the heat of life's hardest moments, He is melting away what doesn't belong, reshaping us, refining us, and making us into something more beautiful than we ever imagined.

Parenting a child through mental health struggles often feels like standing in a glass making furnace: unbearably hot, overwhelming, and like everything is completely out of our control.

But, just as a master glassblower knows exactly how long to leave the glass in the fire, God knows exactly what we need to go through to be refined, to be made stronger, to be transformed.

Let's be honest: Some of us (myself included) are like stubborn little chunks of glass that refuse to melt gracefully.

But He keeps working on us, shaping us, even when we resist.

God is With You in the Fire—Just Like Shadrach, Meshach, and Abednego

There's something powerful about knowing that God doesn't just send us through the fire—He steps into it with us.

One of my favorite Bible stories is about Shadrach, Meshach, and Abednego—three young men who were thrown into a blazing furnace because they refused to bow down to an idol.

King Nebuchadnezzar ordered them to be burned alive, expecting them to be consumed instantly. But instead of perishing in the flames, something miraculous happened.

"Look! I see four men walking around in the fire, unbound and unharmed, and the fourth looks like a son of the gods." (Daniel 3:25 NIV)

You Are Not Alone in the Fire

They weren't alone in the flames. And neither are you.

Warrior Mom, I know this journey has felt like a blazing inferno: relentless, exhausting, unbearable at times.

You may feel like the heat is too much, like you are on the verge of breaking.

But hear this: God is right there with you.

The very fire that should have consumed you will become the fire that refines you.

The Fire That Sets You Free

Do you know the most incredible part of this story?

When Shadrach, Meshach, and Abednego stepped out of the fire, not a single hair on their heads was singed.

The only thing the fire burned away was the ropes that had bound them.

Let that sink in.

The fire wasn't meant to destroy them. It was meant to set them free.

Your Story is Not Over—You Are Being Refined for a Greater Purpose

Your pain is not wasted.

Every hardship you've endured, every sleepless night you've suffered, every tear you've cried—it all serves a purpose.

God is using this season to prepare you for something greater.

He is shaping you into the Warrior Mom you were always meant to be.

This fire is teaching you some important lessons:

- **Perseverance**—You are learning how to fight—not just for your child but for yourself.
- **Faith**—You are deepening your trust in God in ways you never have before.
- **Strength**—You are being prepared for something bigger than this moment.

One day, another mom will sit where you are now, wondering if she has the strength to keep going.

And because of what you've been through, you will be able to reach out your hand and say, "I see you. I've been there. You're not alone."

"And we know that in all things God works for the good of those who love Him, who have been called according to His purpose." (Romans 8:28 NIV)

Next Step: Step Into the Refining Process

Write down three ways you've already seen growth in yourself through this process. Hold on to them as proof that God is at work.

The Warrior Mom Battle Plan

Now that we've walked through the fire, it's time to step into strength.

In the next chapter, we'll create a battle plan to help you move forward with confidence, faith, and a renewed sense of purpose.

Are you ready? Let's do this, Warrior Mom.

CHAPTER 9

THE WARRIOR MOM BATTLE PLAN

(Phase 5: Purpose and Transformation—The Transformation and Coaching Connection)

Taking the Next Step in Your Warrior Mom Journey

You've walked through the fire.

You've faced heartbreak, fear, uncertainty, and yet, you are still standing.

You're stronger than you ever thought possible, because every tear, every late-night prayer, and every battle you've fought has built a strength within you that cannot be shaken.

You're wiser than you were when this battle began, because through the heartbreak, the setbacks, and the moments you thought you couldn't go on, you've gained a depth of knowledge and understanding that only comes from walking through the fire.

You're more resilient than you ever imagined, because despite the pain, despite the fear, despite the nights when you wondered if you could keep going, you *did*. And you're still standing, not just as a survivor, but as a Warrior Mom who refuses to give up.

But this is not the end of your journey.

This is the beginning of a new way of living—one where you are no longer reacting to every crisis but standing firm in faith, strategy, and resilience.

A warrior doesn't just show up to battle unprepared.

She has a battle plan.

And that's exactly what we are going to build together.

Beauty from Ashes: Chloe's Thriving Journey

While parts of our story have been incredibly hard, there is light. Beauty has risen from the ashes. As of my writing this book, Chloe is a thriving, happy seventeen-year-old girl. She has rediscovered her joy and purpose in ways that remind me daily of God's faithfulness.

Chloe recently got her first job at a doggie daycare—a perfect fit for the ultimate animal whisperer. She has always had a unique way with animals, and now she gets to spend her days surrounded by them, feeling fulfilled and confident in her abilities. It's incredible to watch her step into something she loves, gaining independence and purpose along the way.

Academically, she is excelling in her junior year of homeschool high school, finding a rhythm that works for her. Without the pressures of a traditional school environment, she has been able to succeed on her own terms in a way that supports both her learning style and her mental well-being.

And let's not forget—she is driving now. Lord, help us. Every time she gets behind the wheel, I have to remind myself that God is in control. And, of course, wherever she goes, her precious service dog, Luna, is always with her.

Luna plays an essential role in Chloe's continued healing. In stressful or overwhelming situations, Luna provides comfort and grounding, helping Chloe navigate anxiety and giving her the reassurance she needs to face the world. This dog is more than just a pet—she is a lifeline, a steady presence in the storms, and a reminder that Chloe is never alone.

This transformation—from despair to hope, from pain to purpose—is proof that the battle is worth fighting. And just as Chloe has learned to embrace her healing journey, it's time for you to step into yours.

The Healing Process is Messy, But Worth It

Listen, I know what you're thinking: *That sounds nice, but my life is still a dumpster fire.*

Trust me, I get it.

There were days when I felt like I was drowning in exhaustion, fueled only by caffeine and sheer determination.

But here's what I learned:

- Every small step forward matters.

- Chloe didn't wake up one day magically healed, and neither will you.
- Healing is messy and nonlinear, and it sometimes feels like taking two steps forward and one step back.

The key is to keep moving.

Finding the Right Support

Therapy, counseling, and support groups can be game-changers. But too often, we hesitate. We tell ourselves we should be able to handle it. That, as moms, we should be strong enough to figure it out on our own.

But true strength isn't about doing it alone—it's about knowing when to reach out for help.

For Chloe, finding the right counselor wasn't just about therapy—it was about having someone who could truly see her, guide her, and remind her of the progress she was making.

I will never forget the moment when her counselor looked at her and said, "You did it."

She had done the hard, uncomfortable, soul-wrenching work of processing her trauma through EMDR therapy.

And now? She had overcome it.

For the first time in what felt like forever, Chloe smiled—truly smiled. And in her eyes, I saw real joy.

Her brain had finally begun healing from the trauma.

Tears welled up in my own eyes as I watched her take in the moment. This was what we had fought for.

The sleepless nights. The countless therapy sessions. The prayers whispered in desperation.

It was all leading to this—healing, hope, and breakthrough.

If you are in the middle of the storm, hold on to this truth: Healing is possible. It doesn't happen overnight, but God is still working, even in the waiting.

The Warrior Mom Mindset—This Battle is Holy Work

You, Warrior Mom, are doing holy work.

Your battle scars tell a story of resilience, grit, and love so deep it defies words.

Your late nights, prayers whispered through tears, unwavering presence in your child's life—it all matters.

This isn't just about your child's healing.

You're stepping into *your* healing, too.

This journey is about more than just survival—it's about transformation.

Learning to live fully again. Embracing joy without guilt. Reclaiming your own identity while still being the fierce protector your child needs.

And let me tell you, *it's absolutely worth it.*

Setting Faith Goals: Walking in Purpose and Strength

Every warrior needs a mission—a clear vision for where she is headed. Faith goals help you:

- Anchor yourself in God's truth.
- Set intentional steps forward.
- Refuse to stay stuck in survival mode.

How to Set Faith-Based Goals

- **Identify Your Core Priorities**—What matters most to you as a mom? Your child's healing? Your own healing? Spiritual growth? Emotional stability? Write it down.
- **Align Your Goals with God's Word**—For example, if fear has been controlling you, your goal might be to walk in faith daily, using 2 Timothy 1:7 (BSB) as an anchor: *"For God has not given us a spirit of fear, but of power, love, and self-control."*
- **Make Them Actionable**—Instead of saying, *"I want to trust God more,"* say, *"I will start each morning with prayer and declare God's promises over my child before I even get out of bed."*
- **Celebrate Progress, Not Perfection**—Growth happens step by step, not all at once. Give yourself grace.
- **Prioritize Self-Care**—A healthy mom is an effective mom. Schedule time for prayer, journaling, exercise, and rest. Taking care of yourself fuels your ability to show up strong for your child.

- **Surround Yourself with Support**—No warrior fights alone. Find community through a church group, support network, or trusted friends. Isolation fuels exhaustion, but community brings strength.

- **Practice Gratitude and Reflection**—Write down three things you're grateful for daily. Gratitude shifts perspective, reminding you that even in the struggle, God is working.

- **Speak Life Over Yourself and Your Child**—Your words have power. Declare truth over fear, faith over doubt. For example, *"God is healing my child. I am equipped for this battle. We are walking in victory."*

Action Step: Write Your Faith-Based Goals

Write down three faith-based goals that will guide you in this next season. Keep them somewhere visible.

Every time you doubt your progress, return to these goals and remind yourself that you are walking in victory.

The Final Charge—You Were Chosen for This Fight

In our final chapter, we will step into full empowerment.

You are not the same woman who started this book.

You are stronger. You are wiser. And you are ready to step into the calling of a Warrior Mom.

Let's finish strong.

CHAPTER 10

THE FINAL CHARGE—YOU WERE CHOSEN FOR THIS FIGHT

(Phase 5: Purpose and Transformation—The Transformation and Coaching Connection)

Stepping Fully Into Your Calling as a Warrior Mom

Warrior Mom, take a deep breath.

Let this sink in—you have walked through fire (or are still walking through it). You have fought battles both seen and unseen. And yet, you are still standing.

Not only that, but you are stronger, wiser, and more equipped than when you first began this journey.

But this is not the end.

This is the beginning of stepping fully into who God created you to be.

There was a time when I never thought I'd see the day when peace would feel normal again, when joy would return to my home, or when Chloe would be thriving instead of just surviving. Yet, here we are. And if God can do it for my family, He can do it for yours.

Esther's Courage: Walking Boldly Into Your Purpose

As you step forward into this next season, I want you to remember the story of Queen Esther.

Esther never sought the throne. She was an ordinary Jewish girl thrust into an extraordinary role. When she became queen, she had no idea that one day, she would be called to risk everything.

A decree had been issued to annihilate her people. She was their only hope. But stepping into the king's court uninvited? That could cost her life.

She had every reason to hesitate:

- Fear gripped her.
- She felt unqualified.
- She questioned if she had the strength.

Yet Mordecai's words changed everything: *"Who knows but that you have come to your royal position for such a time as this?"* (Esther 4:14 NIV)

This wasn't about status. It wasn't about comfort. It was about purpose.

So, she made her choice.

- She sought God first—fasting and praying for wisdom.

- She stepped forward in faith—choosing courage over comfort.
- She surrendered the outcome—trusting God with what she couldn't control.

And because of her obedience, her people were saved.

"I will go to the king… And if I perish, I perish." (Esther 4:16 NIV)

Her bravery changed history.

You Were Chosen for This Fight

Warrior Mom, you are no different from Esther.

You may feel unqualified. You may be afraid. You may wonder if you are strong enough for this battle.

But let me remind you: God did not place you in this season by accident. God does not call the qualified—He equips the ones He has called.

You were chosen to be your child's mother.

You were placed in this battle for a reason.

You have been called for such a time as this.

And just like Esther, you are not alone. God goes before you. He fights for you. He equips you.

Walking in Personal Growth and Transformation

Your journey doesn't end here. Healing is not a destination—it's a lifelong commitment.

As Warrior Moms, we are not just fighting for our children's well-being. We are called to grow, to evolve, and to lead by example. Because the truth is you cannot lead your child to healing if you are unwilling to grow yourself.

Why Your Growth Matters

Your healing impacts your child's healing. When you choose to strengthen your faith, build resilience, and step into wholeness, your child watches. They learn that healing is possible because they see it in you.

You have the power to break generational cycles. Pain, fear, and survival-mode parenting don't have to be your legacy. When you commit to growth, you shift the patterns in your family. You become the example of wisdom, faith, and perseverance instead of reaction and exhaustion.

Growth builds confidence and resilience. When you invest in your personal development—spiritually, emotionally, and mentally—you strengthen your mindset. You begin to lead with peace instead of panic, wisdom instead of fear.

Warrior Mom, your transformation isn't just for you—it's the foundation for your family's future.

So, keep going. Keep growing. Keep stepping into the woman God is calling you to be. Because as you rise, you bring your family with you.

Keep Growing—and Get Support When You Need It

Personal growth is powerful, but let's be real—this journey takes a toll.

Remember to Seek Counseling for Yourself if Needed

This battle isn't just hard on our kids. It's hard on us, too. And sometimes, *we* need support. Whether it's personal counseling or family therapy, getting the right help can be a game-changer.

I'll be the first to admit it: I have PTSD from this journey. Every time I can't get in touch with Chloe on the first try? Sheer panic. My heart races, my mind spirals, and I go straight to worst-case scenarios.

But then I pause, take a deep breath, and remind myself of the truth.

I literally say it out loud: "You are a princess of the Most High God—so straighten your crown and act like it."

Warrior Mom, this fight is real. But you don't have to fight it alone. Get the support you need—because healing isn't just for your child. It's for you, too.

Your Next Steps: Walking Boldly as a Warrior Mom

Now that you've completed this journey, you may be wondering: *What's next? How do I continue to grow, strengthen my faith, and lead my child well?*

Here are your next steps:

- **Commit to Daily Prayer and Scripture**—Your strength will always come from God. Make it a priority to spend time in His presence every day.

- **Find a Community**—You are not meant to do this alone. Find a support group, a Warrior Mom coaching program, or a circle of faith-filled women who will lift you up.

- **Continue Your Own Healing**—If you haven't sought counseling or support for yourself, now is the time. Your healing is just as important as your child's.

- **Take Care of Your Mind, Body, and Spirit**—Self-care is not optional; it is a survival strategy. Make time for rest, hobbies, and activities that bring you joy.

- **Be an Encourager**—Share what you've learned. Speak life into other moms who are walking this road. What God has done in you, He can do in others.

- **Keep Believing for Your Child**—Even if you don't see the progress you want yet, don't give up. God is still working, and a breakthrough is coming.

Scripture Tie-In: Strength for the Journey

"I can do all things through Christ who strengthens me." (Philippians 4:13 NKJV)

Warrior Mom, you were made for this.

This is your Esther moment. Step forward boldly, trusting that God has already gone before you.

This is not the end of your journey. This is the beginning of your boldest chapter yet.

Final Step: Declare Your Faith and Walk Boldly

Write down one declaration of faith that you will carry forward from this book. Speak it daily, believe it fully, and walk boldly into the future God has prepared for you.

FINAL THOUGHTS

This is not the end of your story. This is the beginning of a new season. A season of hope, of healing, and of stepping fully into the calling God has placed on your life.

The refining fire did not destroy you, Warrior Mom. It made you stronger. It made you ready. Now, walk forward in faith, knowing that the same God who carried you through this journey will continue to guide you in the days ahead.

If you're still in the trenches, keep going.

Keep praying, keep advocating, and keep speaking life over your child.
Keep standing when you want to collapse, and keep laughing when you want to cry.
Keep showing up, even on the days when you don't feel like enough. (Spoiler alert: You are enough!)

A breakthrough is coming.

If you've walked through the fire and made it to the other side, don't keep the journey to yourself.

There's another mom out there drowning in guilt, fear, and exhaustion. She needs what you've learned.

Be the support you once prayed for. Send the text. Make the call. Share your story.

Remind her that she is not alone.

Your Next Steps

- **Keep Growing**—Stay in the Word, stay in therapy (yes, that, too), and keep making your own healing a priority.
- **Find your People**—You were never meant to do this alone. Surround yourself with Warrior Moms who will lift you up (and remind you to drink water).
- **Make a Battle Plan**—Set intentional goals for your parenting, faith, and advocacy. Hope is not a strategy—get practical.
- **Pray like a Warrior**—Cover your child in prayer, not just when things are hard, but daily. Speak life over them, even when they roll their eyes at you.

This battle has shaped you.

It has strengthened you, not destroyed you.

It has refined you, not defeated you.

It has equipped you for what's ahead.

So stand up, Warrior Mom. Adjust your armor. Step into this next season with faith, fire, and an unshakable belief that God is working, even in the unseen.

Go forward with confidence. There is purpose in your pain and beauty in your story.

Scripture to Hold On To:

"I can do all things through Christ who strengthens me." (Philippians 4:13 NKJV)

WARRIOR MOM, RISE!

D ear Warrior Mom,

Take a deep breath. Feel the weight of what you've carried.

The sleepless nights. The battles you've fought in hospital rooms, in school offices, and behind closed doors. The prayers you've whispered through tears. The exhaustion that runs so deep you don't even know who you are anymore.

I see you.

I know what it's like to wonder if you're strong enough to do this. To sit in the car after another impossible appointment, gripping the steering wheel, trying to breathe. To beg God for answers, for a breakthrough, for just *one* moment of peace. To feel like no one else understands this kind of love—the kind that breaks you and builds you all at once.

And I need you to hear me:

- You were made for this.
- You are *not* here by accident.
- You were *chosen* to fight for your child.

Not because you have all the answers. Not because you're perfect. Not because you're never afraid.

But because God knew you would rise.

- He knew you would fight when the world said, "Give up."
- He knew you would stand when everything tried to break you.
- He knew you would love your child fiercely—through the storm, through the darkness, through the unknown.

And He knew that even in the moments when you wanted to quit, you wouldn't give up.

A Call to Rise

I won't lie to you: This road is brutal.

It will take everything you have. And then it will ask for more.

But hear me: You are stronger than you know.

Because strength isn't never breaking.

Strength is breaking and getting back up anyway.

- Strength is sitting in a waiting room, terrified, but showing up anyway.
- Strength is standing up for your child when people dismiss their pain.
- Strength is choosing hope—again and again—when fear tells you to quit.

I know you're tired. I know you're weary.

But I also know this: You are NOT done.

A Testimony of Hope

There was a time I thought the darkness would swallow us whole.

I couldn't see the light. I couldn't imagine a future where Chloe was *okay*. I thought I would drown in the weight of it all.

But we made it through.

And if God can do it for my family, He can do it for yours.

Every tear, every prayer, every fight—He has seen it all, and He has been equipping you through every single battle.

I can't promise the road will be easy. But I can promise you this: You were never meant to fight alone. God is in this with you, and He is *not* finished with you or your child.

Warrior Mom, Straighten Your Crown

You are a Warrior.
You are stronger than the storm.
You are walking in victory, even when you feel defeated.
You are not fighting alone—God is with you.

So lift your head. Square your shoulders. Straighten your crown.

And *rise*.

The world needs you. Your child needs you.

You will fight, *Warrior Mom*. And in the end, with His grace, you will win.

With love, fierce belief, and warrior pride,

Jenn

Scripture to Hold On To:

"She is clothed with strength and dignity; she can laugh at the days to come." (Proverbs 31:25)

STAY CONNECTED–THE JOURNEY CONTINUES!

- **Join the Warrior Mom Coaching Community**—Get access to support groups, live calls, and additional resources.
- **Download the Warrior Mom Toolkits**—Use these tools to help you track your progress and stay grounded in faith.
- **Stay in Touch**—Follow me on social media or visit my website, warriormomcoach.net, for ongoing encouragement and resources.
- **Book a Call with Me**—Visit my website to book a call with me. This is a free call to determine how I can best be of support to you.
- **Purchase the 30-day Warrior Mom Devotional**—Visit warriormomcoach.net to help you dive into your faith.

From the bottom of my heart, thank you for allowing me to walk this journey with you.

This is not the end. This is just the beginning.

Go forward, Warrior Mom. The best is yet to come.